starting with STEAM

SPACE EXPLORERS

Annette Gulati

Rourke Educational Media
A Division of Carson Dellosa Education
rourkeeducationalmedia.com

ROURKE'S
SCHOOL to HOME
CONNECTIONS

BEFORE AND DURING READING ACTIVITIES

Before Reading: *Building Background Knowledge and Vocabulary*

Building background knowledge can help children process new information and build upon what they already know. Before reading a book, it is important to tap into what children already know about the topic. This will help them develop their vocabulary and increase their reading comprehension.

Questions and Activities to Build Background Knowledge:

1. Look at the front cover of the book and read the title. What do you think this book will be about?
2. What do you already know about this topic?
3. Take a book walk and skim the pages. Look at the table of contents, photographs, captions, and bold words. Did these text features give you any information or predictions about what you will read in this book?

Vocabulary: *Vocabulary Is Key to Reading Comprehension*

Use the following directions to prompt a conversation about each word.

- Read the vocabulary words.
- What comes to mind when you see each word?
- What do you think each word means?

Vocabulary Words:

- *comets*
- *data*
- *measure*
- *planets*
- *satellites*
- *technology*

During Reading: *Reading for Meaning and Understanding*

To achieve deep comprehension of a book, children are encouraged to use close reading strategies. During reading, it is important to have children stop and make connections. These connections result in deeper analysis and understanding of a book.

Close Reading a Text

During reading, have children stop and talk about the following:

- Any confusing parts
- Any unknown words
- Text to text, text to self, text to world connections
- The main idea in each chapter or heading

Encourage children to use context clues to determine the meaning of any unknown words. These strategies will help children learn to analyze the text more thoroughly as they read.

When you are finished reading this book, turn to the last page for an **After Reading Activity**.

Table of Contents

What's Out There?

Space is far, far away.
What's happening out there?

Earth

Scientists help us learn about space. They study Earth and other **planets**.

They study the sun and the moon.
They study **comets** and stars.

Amazing Machines

Engineers use **technology** to help scientists.

Rockets take scientists to space.

Robots collect samples. **Satellites** take pictures. Telescopes do too!

Numbers and Pictures

Scientists use math to study space. They gather **data.** They make graphs.

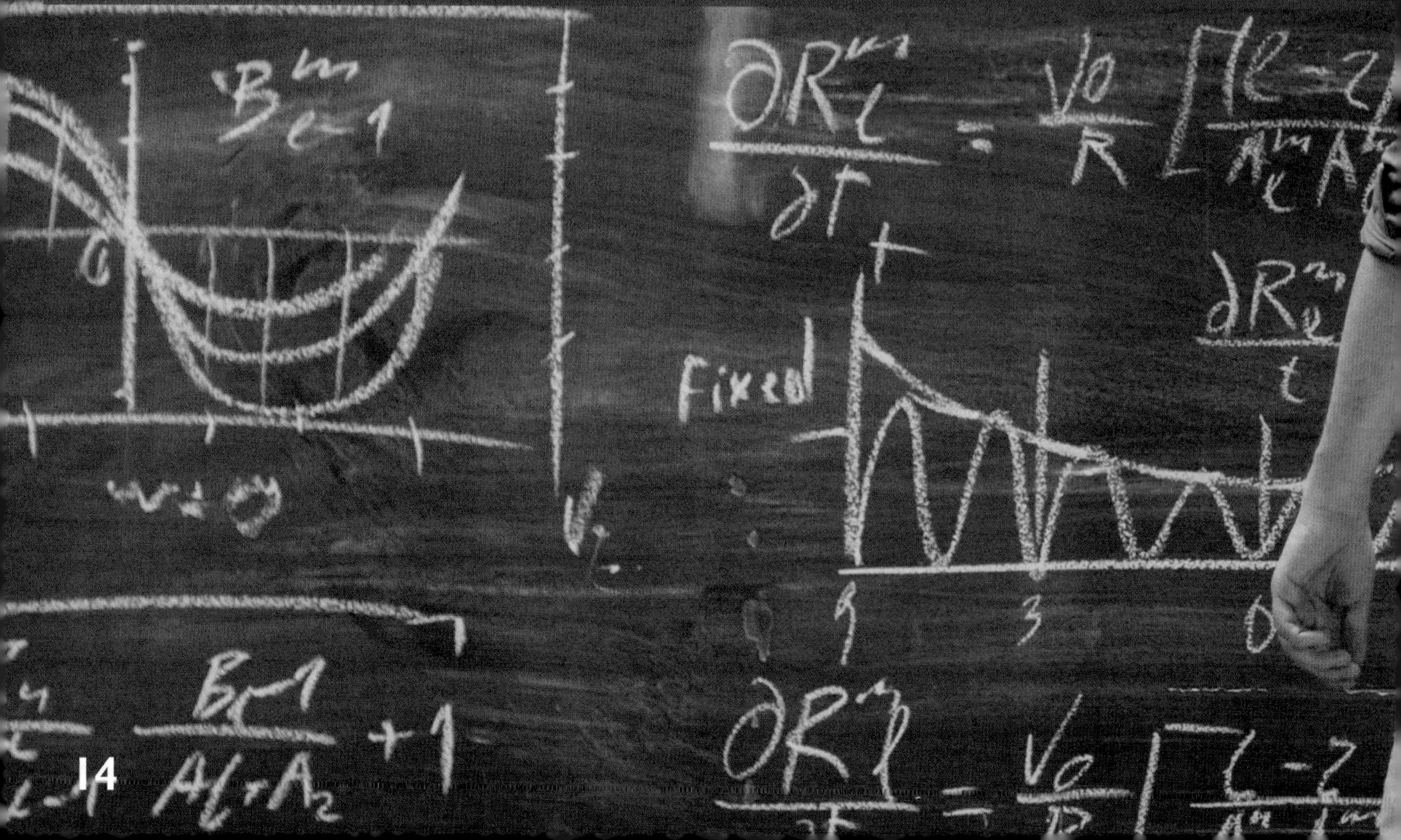

They **measure** distances.
They measure speeds.

Artists help us see what space is like. They draw and paint pictures of space. They make sculptures too.

Many people help us learn about space.

Make A Model Spaceship

Make a model spaceship. Then, decide if your spaceship needs a door, a window, a camera, or something else. Use more materials to make these details for your ship.

You will need:

- ✓ potato chip canister
- ✓ foil
- ✓ glue

- ✓ cardboard
- ✓ scissors
- ✓ construction paper

Directions:

1. Cover the chip canister with foil. Glue it in place.
2. Make fins out of cardboard. Glue them on the spaceship body.
3. Make a cone out of paper. Glue it on top of your spaceship.

Photo Glossary

comets (KAH-mits): Long-tailed chunks of dust and ice that travel around the sun.

data (DAY-tuh): Facts and information collected for study.

measure (MEZH-ur): To figure out the size or weight of something.

planets (PLAN-its): Large natural objects that travel around a star such as our sun.

satellites (SAT-uh-lites): Devices that are sent into space to collect and send information.

technology (tek-NAH-luh-jee): Machines and equipment developed through science and engineering.

Index

After Reading Activity

Pick a planet that interests you. Learn more about the planet. Draw a picture of what you might find there.

About the Author

Annette Gulati loves exploring the world and learning new things. She loves to write and gaze at the stars from her home in Seattle, Washington.

www.rourkeeducationalmedia.com

PHOTO CREDITS: Cover and Title Page © 3DSculptor; Pg 10, 23 © 3DSculptor; Pg 12, 23 © Vadim Sadovski; Pg 16, 22 © INchendio; Pg 6, 23 © narvikk; Pg 8, 22 © sololos; Pg 14, 22 © gorodenkoff; Pg 3 © LisaAlisa_ill; Pg 4 © alex-mit; Pg 18 © Mordolff

Edited by: Kim Thompson
Cover design by: Rhea Magaro-Wallace
Interior design by: Kathy Walsh

Library of Congress PCN Data

Space Explorers / Annette Gulati
(Starting with STEAM)
ISBN 978-1-73161-417-9 (hard cover)(alk. paper)
ISBN 978-1-73161-212-0 (soft cover)
ISBN 978-1-73161-522-0 (e-Book)
ISBN 978-1-73161-627-2 (ePub)

Library of Congress Control Number: 2019932072

Printed in the United States of America, North Mankato, Minnesota